learn ai with miqa- the robot

your first ai book

by 'bhu'

your first ai book! ever!

this book belongs to ________________

hi!
my name is miqa and i invite
you to learn ai with me in a
fun way!

we will learn ai core concepts;
activities and make some cool
stuff with ai!

hope you will enjoy and learn
so much through the pages
that follow!

contents

"ai" stands for artificial intelligence.

what is artificial?
something that is man made
and not natural.

what is intelligence?
when you think and solve your
problems and learn everyday -
you are intelligent.

yes you are!
learn every day
ask questions; stay curious!

find out what is real and what is artificial on this page

so artificial intelligence is
when a man-made thing
has intelligence-

- it can think.
- it can solve problems.
- it learns everyday.

but it has to be taught.

and who teaches these
machines?
us! humans!

ai is like a brain for computers; machines; and even smart toys!

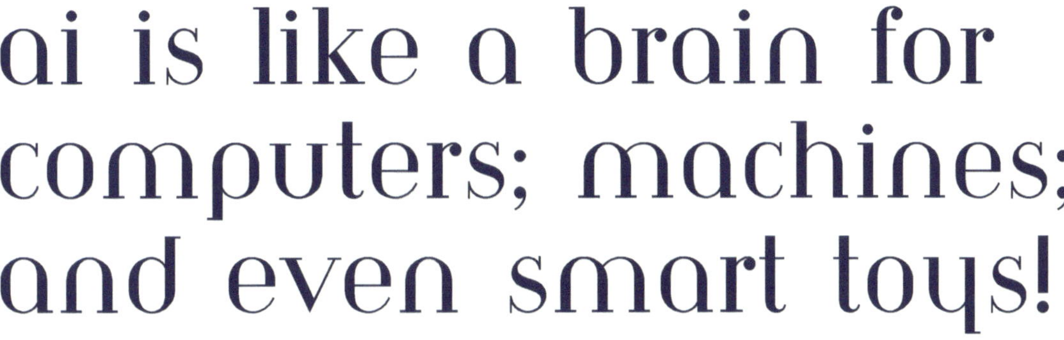

it helps them learn new things; make decisions; and sometimes even talk to us!

ai needs data to learn

- to learn a trick a puppy needs lots of examples! data is like those examples.

- the more a puppy learns; the more it gets trained. more data means ai can understand things better.

- many and good examples help the puppy the most! ai gets trained on huge amount of data.

"curiosity is your
superpower!
the more you ask; the more
you learn!"

so remember to ask
questions every day!

let us learn some core concepts of ai

learning from examples

ai learns by looking at lots of examples and figuring out patterns.

imagine you're trying to teach miqa how to spot a cat. you show it many pictures of cats; and over time; miqa gets better and better at spotting cats all on its own!!

2

trial and error

ai sometimes makes mistakes; but that's okay because it learns from them.

just like when you try to ride a bike and fall; the more you try; the better you get!

ai works the same way—if it gets something wrong; it tries again until it gets it right.

3

ai can recognize things (pattern recognition)

ai can look at pictures; sounds; or data and figure out what they are because it has got training in it.

can you find out what comes next?

4

ai can help in problem solving!

ai can help people do things faster and better!

it can help you pick your favorite songs or even find the quickest way to get to school -anything that is long; tedious or hard to do.

5

ai doesn't have feelings (no emotions)

ai is like a helper robot; miqa.

it knows how to do things; but it doesn't feel happy or sad—it is just really good at what it does.

A

6

ai needs instructions (humans teach ai)

even though ai can do cool things; it still needs humans to tell it what to do and help it learn!

if you tell miqa to sort toys into the right boxes; it'll do it over and over again without getting tired.

7

ai can make predictions

ai is like a wizard who can guess what might happen next!

it can guess if it will rain tomorrow by looking at lots of weather data from the past.

or which netflix movie you will like to watch depending on your watch history.

8

ai can help us be creative

ai can help make new things; like music; stories; or pictures; but it still needs people to add the "magic".

like miqa can help you draw pictures or write songs; but it's your ideas and feelings that make them special.

ai and teamwork

ai is like a super helper; but it still needs a teammate like you to guide it and make sure it's doing the right thing.

wonders happen when human works with ai.

bonus: fun ai superpower
(ai can do many things)

ai is like a superhero with lots of powers; like miqa!

it can help with homework; draw pictures; play games; predict weather; share latest cricket scores; identify new constellations and even clean your room!

activity 1 –
what can ai help you with?

activity 2 –
ai adventure word search

B	R	A	I	N	R	O	B	O	T	S	D	U
I	L	G	C	I	S	C	A	L	H	F	C	S
N	A	T	U	R	A	L	P	Q	E	N	E	A
A	M	A	C	H	I	N	E	L	E	A	R	N
L	L	D	S	E	I	M	N	B	D	I	E	R
E	E	H	D	F	I	B	I	O	F	M	T	U
A	O	Q	R	L	M	C	H	R	U	Q	H	G
R	S	R	P	A	T	T	E	R	N	N	W	W
E	O	I	B	K	J	P	X	E	O	D	S	D
M	A	T	H	B	I	I	Y	S	F	I	M	R
A	L	G	O	R	I	T	H	M	T	U	U	I
R	B	D	H	R	R	I	Q	D	C	S	S	W
I	T	E	E	O	O	M	Y	A	W	S	O	P
N	E	U	R	O	N	T	O	O	W	G	L	N
E	X	A	M	P	L	E	A	D	H	R	O	P

activity 3 -
trace and fill colors in robot

activity 4 -

draw your own ai robot ; list down its superpowers

remember - ai needs our guidance

while ai can be smart; it still needs us (humans) to tell it what's right and wrong.

miqa could accidentally make a mistake if not told properly.

and thats why we need to follow ai ethics

"thanks for going on this adventure with miqa!

keep dreaming big; and remember; with ai; the possibilities are endless!"

some fun ai apps for you to explore -

quickdraw - you draw and object and ai attempts to guess what it is.
(quickdraw.withgoogle.com)

create your own story - you can choose prompts and create your own story.
(whimsyapp.com)

 create pictures with your words - you can prompt ai to create a picture
(craiyon.com)

some fun ai apps for you to try
and learn -

create your music - you can ask what
kind of song you want in text like ' create
a peppy song on starfish' and ai will
create one (suno.ai)

co-create drawing with ai - you can draw
prompts and ai tries to finish your
drawing. (magic-sketchpad.glitch.me)

get your maths answers - you can ask ai
to add up large numbers like 45678 and
34566. (perplexity.ai)